Acknowledgements

Thanks to all my old and new friends
for their support and encouragement during this project.
Special thanks go to Pete Manjuck
for sharing his Feng Shui knowledge and sense of humor,
Julie Zamagni for creating such a beautiful piece of art for the cover,
and Linda Bevard for her editing expertise
and the synchronicities we experienced
while working together.

Feng Shui
For Your Home and Garden

An easy guide for everyone

Erin,
Best wishes for
health, happiness!
& prosperity
Kathy Quinn

Kathleen K. Quinn

HOME AND garden feng shui

Denver Colorado
www.homeandgardenfengshui.com

Visit our website:
www.homeandgardenfengshui.com.

Edited by Linda Bevard
Layout and Design by Karin Hoffman
 A. J. Images, Inc.
Graphic & Communication Design

Cover Art Illustrated by Julie Zamagni
Interior Illustrations by Mary Anne Hendrix
Author Photo by Carissa Brown

Published by Home and Garden Feng Shui LLC
2510 Raleigh Street, Denver, Colorado 80212.
(303) 458-1225.

First printing 2004.

ISBN   0-9749633-0-5

Library of Congress Control Number: 2004101316

Table of Contents

Feng Shui (pronounced "fung shway") literally means *wind and water*. Feng Shui is simply the study of how to arrange your environment to enhance your life. It originated in China thousands of years ago. More and more people are adopting the practice of Feng Shui today as a way to find balance and harmony in our fast-paced and stressful world.

Do you usually arrive home realizing that you have had a great day? Or, perhaps, did you spend your time waiting in traffic, working in a "sick building," performing last-minute changes and rush jobs, and standing in lines?

Our environment affects us on a subconscious level, and so we don't realize how much it may be negatively influencing our lives. Using Feng Shui, you can make a conscious effort to shape an environment that enhances your life. When our environments are properly balanced and we are surrounded with positive energy, we can live richer, fuller, happier lives.

Have you ever walked into a home or garden and instantly felt comfortable and relaxed—or uncomfortable for no apparent reason? An explanation for these positive or negative feelings in different environments may be found in the principles of Feng Shui. Feng Shui is about the conscious and subconscious associations you have with things. Feng Shui doesn't change the situation, but it changes our mind about the situation by using enhancements, cures, and intention.

The ultimate objective of using Feng Shui in your home and garden is to create a sanctuary, a balanced and harmonious place that is supportive to the people who live there. Feng Shui uses symbolism to elicit positive thinking. Once we become aware of how our environment affects us, we can empower it. By placing positive images and objects in our environment, we are activating mental energies that create positive thoughts. If we live in a cluttered environment, we will manifest the same in our mind and will feel stuck in our life. When you let go of objects which are no longer of use to you, your life becomes clearer. Before making any Feng Shui adjustments, you must clear the clutter from your environment.

Feng Shui is not about making drastic changes or purchasing new items, but making energetic improvements in your space. A simple thing such as moving an object you trip over every morning or always keeping your car keys in the same place will reduce the stress in your life.

What you will learn from this book are practical and common-sense ways to improve the quality of your life by using a form of Feng Shui that has been adapted to fit with our contemporary Western lifestyle.

Feng Shui is for everyone. It's a way of life. You will see the world through different eyes after reading this book.

Compass School Versus Form School
(Ancient Versus Modern Feng Shui)

*U*nderstanding Feng Shui is challenging. There are so many different ways of practicing it, and so many books to read, it can leave you even more confused than you were before you started investigating this ancient and fascinating art. It is believed that there are more than 100 schools of Feng Shui.

Each school has its own merits. All are based on the following principle: Place the right objects in the right places to be in harmony and balance with yourself, nature, and the universe. As you do this, you will also activate the areas of your life that you wish to improve: health, love, romance, marriage, children, business, career, creativity, self-development and knowledge, wealth, fame, prosperity, and aspirations.

More than 3,000 years ago in China, the original Feng Shui practitioners used the compass to determine the best directions for homes to face, for sleeping positions, for different kinds of luck, and for protection from the elements. This patriarchal society based its Feng Shui cures on the birth date of the man of the house.

Our style of living has changed significantly since that time. There may not be a man of the house, or the man and woman of the house are considered equals. Who gets to decide which direction the partners sleep in? Or will they have to sleep head to toe?

Also, most of us buy houses that either are already built or are subject to covenants. We don't have the option of choosing which direction our front door faces. The Compass method can, however, be applied if you are building a new home on your own property and have no restrictions.

A basic principle of Feng Shui is that everything is always changing. Feng Shui itself has also changed, so that its ancient principles can be adapted to our contemporary lifestyle. Contemporary Feng Shui recommends arranging objects to achieve optimal energy flow according to a mapping system using the Bagua Map, which determines the location of separate pools of energy associated with nine areas of your life. Much of it is simply good common sense and logic. This book is based on the teachings of the Form School.

If one form of Feng Shui does not give you the results you seek, feel free to try another.

Everything Is Alive. Every single object in our surroundings is "alive" with our memories and associations. Each time we look at an object, we consciously or subconsciously experience associations—where and when we bought it, for example, or who gave it to us. The goal in Feng Shui is to possess only objects that bring about good memories and associations. If we have a piece of furniture or artwork left over from a failed relationship, each time we look at that piece, our energy is drained. Once you let go of the things you no longer love, the more you attract to yourself the things you do love.

Everything Is Connected. Everything in our lives is connected to everything else in our lives. For example, if you sit in an uncomfortable office chair all day, you may end up with a sore back, causing you to be cranky when you get home. This will affect your relationship. You may have to visit your chiropractor, which affects your prosperity. You may have to take time off from work for this doctor visit, and that affects your job.

Everything Is Always Changing. Change is constant, whether we like it or not. You are changing right now as you read this book—you are becoming more knowledgeable about Feng Shui. Everything you experience changes you—taking a vacation, meeting new people, watching your children grow and move on. Don't be afraid of change; look at change as an adventure.

Surround Yourself With Things You Love. This is so simple. If there is an item in your home that you don't love, get rid of it. You get a great feeling of relief when that thing hits the dumpster! If you share your home with someone and you have different opinions about what is beautiful, try to assign spaces for both of you where you can each have your personal treasures on view.

Are you keeping an unwanted gift, a piece of family furniture, or artwork you really don't like but can't bear to throw away? Offer it to a family member or friend who does like it. You'll make their day—and yours.

Consider Comfort and Safety. You may absolutely fall in love with a piece of furniture, but why put it in your home if it's extremely uncomfortable or has sharp edges you bump into? High heels may make your legs look great, but they ruin your feet. Quite simply, don't include things in your life that hurt you.

Chi is energy – good and bad. Beneficial Chi is positive energy found in places that are bright, refreshing and uplifting. Unhealthy or negative Chi is found in disorder, sickness, anger and depression. It can also be a product of unwelcome visitors or unpleasant views. Chi is invisible and flows like the wind. It likes to move through your home as though it were a gentle breeze or a meandering stream. Where it is blocked, the energy becomes stagnant. Where nothing intervenes to slow it down, it rushes right through your space.

In Feng Shui, the goal is to harness positive Chi and minimize negative Chi. It should be encouraged to flow in and around each space. The flow of Chi is enhanced by mirrors, plants, screens, crystals, lights, water features, and animals. These are some tips for improving the flow of Chi in your surroundings:

- Open windows and doors to encourage the circulation of fresh air.

- Pull back the curtains and allow the sunshine in.

- In general, choose light colors over dark and curves over sharp lines.

- Use natural materials—100 percent cotton sheets, wool, and down—rather than artificial fibers.

- Choose handmade products over mass-produced items.

- Live simply.

- Follow your intuition.

- Decorate your home with living things—plants, animals, family, friends—to create positive energy.

- Discard, sell, or give away anything that holds negative associations. Only keep things that are useful or that you really love.

- Think positively.

Yin

Yang
Masculine
Active Light
Sun Sky
Hot Hard High
Geometric
Fire

Feminine Passive
Dark Moon
Earth Cold
Soft Low
Floral
Water

Yin and Yang are two opposing yet complementary forces. You've seen the symbol. A circle is divided into two sinuous halves, one of them black (Yin) and incorporating a small white circle (Yang); the other side white, or Yang, with a small black Yin circle. This representation reminds us that each force incorporates an element of its opposite. The opposite characteristics of Yin and Yang create energy and maintain balance. Feng Shui is about the balance of these opposite energies.

Yin energy is soft, feminine, passive, quiet, and dark. It can be represented by floral fabrics, ornate objects, and curves. In your home, a plush sofa has Yin qualities; in your garden, the hammock is Yin.

Yang energy is hard, masculine, bright, and loud and can be represented by vertical stripes, geometric patterns, bold colors, and squares. A wooden bench has Yang qualities, as does a barbecue.

In addition to Yin and Yang, Feng Shui uses symbolic representations of the productive and destructive cycles of the five elements—water, wood, fire, earth, and metal—to make modifications in your home or yard. Each element can be represented by a color or shape, or you can incorporate the element itself.

- FIRE is represented by the color red, flames, candles, barbecues, stoves, and lighting. People and animals are also associated with the fire element.

- EARTH is represented by stones, sand, clay, ceramics, pottery, and soil. The colors are brown, beige, neutral, yellow, or terra-cotta.

- METAL is represented by the actual metals or their colors: silver, gold, copper, chrome, aluminum, iron, bronze, pewter, steel, rocks, stones, flagstone, concrete, slate, and granite.

- WATER is represented by aquariums, water features, ponds, and fountains. The associated color is black or very dark blue.

- WOOD is represented by actual wood, wicker, bamboo, books, magazines, and the color green.

Productive Cycle

Water grows wood
Wood provides fuel for fire
Ashes from fire create earth
Earth creates metal
Metal produces water

Destructive Cycle

Water extinguishes fire
Fire melts metal
Metal (ax) cuts wood
Wood consumes earth
Earth dams water

The elements have two separate relationships. The first is productive: Water nourishes wood; wood provides fuel for fire; fire's ashes create earth; earth creates metal; and metal produces water (condensation). The second relationship, the destructive cycle, shows how one element can overcome or be destroyed by the other. That is, water extinguishes fire; fire melts metal; metal (e.g., an ax) cuts wood; wood displaces or consumes earth; earth dams water.

Feng Shui seeks to harmonize the space by balancing the elements in each room. Where there is a predominance of one element, others are introduced to achieve balance.

Before you begin placing Feng Shui cures or enhancements in your home or yard, you must clear the clutter and start with a clean space. Living in a clutter-free environment brings you greater clarity and energy, and it also makes room for new and better things.

Start by examining your environment. Do you feel happy when you arrive at your home? Which rooms are your favorites? Which ones do you avoid? Why? Is this the ideal environment you want to live in? How do you feel about each object in your home?

*C*lutter is anything unfinished, unused, unresolved, broken, or disorganized. Clutter is those items in our surroundings that have no home of their own. Clutter creates stagnation and a lack of energy in our spaces and in our minds.

Things that we love, use, and appreciate have vibrant energy around them, and that energy extends to us. When we are surrounded with things we don't love, things that bring back negative memories or are no longer useful, we lack focus and direction.

Clutter drains psychic energy. It makes you feel tired and lethargic, keeps you in the past, causes disharmony, makes you procrastinate, can depress you, creates excess baggage, necessitates extra cleaning, makes you disorganized, and distracts you from important things.

Chi can't flow freely through a cluttered home or office. It doesn't move easily around too much furniture in a small space, and it stagnates where it finds accumulated dirt, cobwebs, discarded items, junk, and disorganization of any kind.

> ### How Do I Know If It's Clutter?
>
> Ask yourself these three questions:
> Do I love it?
> Is it genuinely useful?
> Does it lift my energy when I think about it?
> Unless you can answer yes at least once, it's clutter!

Before you make any Feng Shui enhancements, the single most important thing to do is to clear all the clutter from your home. There is no place to hide clutter. If you hide it in the basement, it clutters your subconscious mind. If you pile it in the attic, it limits possibilities in your life—there's no room for movement upward.

Keeping clutter has emotional roots. Acknowledge to yourself that clearing out your clutter will involve some emotional risk. The past is over. Don't be afraid to throw something away that you think you might need some day. Just trust that an equal or better item will be available and that you will have the resources to obtain it. Keeping

Collectibles Versus Clutter

It's okay to treasure collectibles and have possessions. This isn't clutter! How they are displayed or where we store them determines whether the energy they are emitting is supportive or stagnant. It's important to remember that you always need to honor and take care of the things you collect, and their energy will support you.

things against an uncertain future reveals a lack of faith in the ability of the universe to provide what you need at the time you need it. The future isn't here yet. Hanging on to things "just in case" you may need them in the future stagnates your life now.

For example, if you have trouble getting rid of clothes that no longer fit, you may not be accepting your current shape and lack of fitness. If you can't bear to remove the possessions remaining after a loved one has died, it may mean you still have work to do to come to terms with your loss and grief.

The space you create by releasing clutter will allow all kinds of spiritual and emotional gifts—not just material gifts—to flow into your life.

Once you start to look for clutter, you'll see it everywhere: at the main entrance and back door, behind doors, in passageways, under your deck, in the shed and garage, in the car, in filing cabinets and closets, in (and on top of) the refrigerator, under the bed, under the kitchen sink, in the laundry room, in and on your desk, in your bookshelves . . .

Look for:

- Physical dirt, dust, grease
- Things you no longer use
- Too many things in too small a space
- Books and magazines you've read. Unless you are planning to read them again, donate them to a senior citizens' center or women's shelter. People seem to have an extremely hard time parting with books for some reason.
- Newspapers and magazines you haven't had time to read
- Anything that has a negative association or memory
- Anything broken
- Unwanted gifts
- Old downloads, cluttered desktop, saved e-mails, and disorganized files computer files
- Old accounting records
- Outdated study materials
- Letters and phone calls that need to be answered
- Photos that didn't develop properly and their negatives. Invest in a digital camera and keep photos on your computer instead of in piles. Print out only your

Mental and Emotional Clutter

Clutter is not just physical. Here are some examples of mental and emotional clutter:
- Too many things on your calendar
- Overwork
- Worry
- Stress
- Gossip
- Unresolved relationships
- People who drain your energy

favorites. You won't have to buy film or pay for developing.

- Unfinished craft projects
- Clothes you no longer fit into, that are out of style, or that you haven't worn in a year
- Clutter belonging to others
- Piles of laundry
- Doors that squeak or are stuck
- Expired prescriptions and other health products
- Food past its expiration date
- Makeup more than a year old
- Anything stopping doors from opening fully
- Business card collections
- Leaky faucets
- All those sample bottles of shampoo you've brought back from hotels (give them to a homeless shelter)
- Anything you have to maneuver around to get to what you want
- Expired coupons
- Duplicates of anything
- Junk mail
- Grocery bags
- Socks with holes
- Worn-out underwear
- Travel literature
- Old Christmas and greeting cards you've received

And there is clutter in your outdoor space:

- Things you no longer use
- Anything that has a negative association or memory
- Anything broken
- Unfinished projects
- Gates that squeak or are stuck
- Overgrown shrubs
- Plants spaced too closely
- Leaky faucets
- Weeds
- Debris
- Fallen leaves
- Broken branches
- Clogged pond filter
- Anything you have to maneuver around to get to what you want

It's easier to learn to control clutter if you live alone. If there are other people living with you, you will have to educate them. The best way to deal with their clutter is to set a good example. You may actually inspire them. If you are storing other people's clutter in your garage, basement, or attic, give them a call and tell them it's time to come pick it up.

Controlling Clutter

To keep clutter under control, remember this each time you pick something up: If it takes less than 10 seconds to put something away, put it away!

Set achievable goals. Instead of trying to de-clutter your entire home or yard, start small—your wallet or purse, your medicine cabinet, the junk drawer. Outside, the first step is to remove debris, prune dead branches, weed, and repair broken items. Start small, with your patio or a flower bed. You'll be amazed at how your energy changes as things are cleared. This will give you the motivation to move on to a bigger project.

Get five boxes, and as you make your way through the medicine cabinet, closet, or patio, place items in the appropriate boxes:

- Trash
- Repairs (things you are sure you need and will repair)
- Recycling (things to sell or give away)
- Relocate (things to go to another room or another person)
- Dilemma (should I keep?)

> ## Dont Use these Excuses!
>
> It might come back in style.
> I might need it some day.
> But it was a gift!
> It's been in the family for a long time.

Recycling encompasses a large area. You may accumulate a few boxes full of items that will bring you some extra cash at a garage sale. Or you can donate the items to your church or synagogue for the next rummage sale, to thrift shops (their trucks make regular runs through most neighborhoods), or to consignment shops. Senior centers and kids' programs can always use donations.

Clearing clutter will simplify your life, replace chaos with serenity, add time to your day, and release emotional attachments. When you choose to surround yourself with only those things you love, you will begin to create a space that resonates with vibrant energy that supports and nurtures you. The next step in this process is to apply the principles of Feng Shui to your space.

Space Clearing

Space clearing is a ceremonial method of removing negative energy from a room or structure and replacing it with a healthy flow of energy. You may want to do a space clearing any time the energy has changed in a room. A good time to do a space clearing is after an unwanted visitor has been in your home or after an argument, an illness, divorce, or death. Clearing the air in your space of stagnant unhealthy, negative, and unhappy energy allows you to release any pain, suffering, sorrow, and discomfort, and you can start over.

Here are instructions for a powerful space-clearing procedure:

Place 1/8 cup Epsom salts in a heat-proof container. Cover with rubbing alcohol. Light the mixture on fire and let it burn out. Dispose of the salt.

Use this procedure in each room of your home. You will notice that in rooms containing lots of negative energy, the salt and alcohol mixture burns longer.

Please use extreme caution when performing this procedure.

The octagonal Bagua Map contains eight sections or *guas* surrounding the center and is considered the "energy map of Feng Shui." The map is used to identify which parts of your home or yard affect which aspects of your life. In Feng Shui, it is believed that when each of these areas is properly identified and enhanced, your good fortune is strengthened. If you want to improve a certain part of your life, add the color, element, or shape associated with each Bagua area to the corresponding area of your home or garden.

The Bagua is overlaid on a plan of your home with the bottom edge aligned along the wall that contains your front door. You may "stretch" the octagon into a square or rectangle to fit your space. You can apply the Bagua to the house as a whole, to each room, and to any surface in the house (your desk, a bureau). Outside, you can apply the Bagua Map to your entire property, to the front and back yards individually, and to surfaces such as a patio table. Outside, align the Bagua's bottom edge along the entrance to your property.

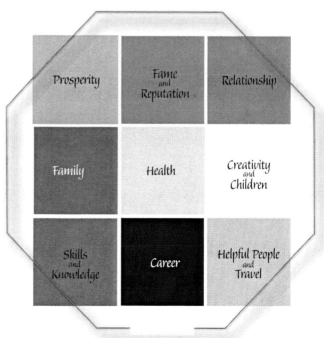

Bagua Map showing names of areas, colors, shapes and elements

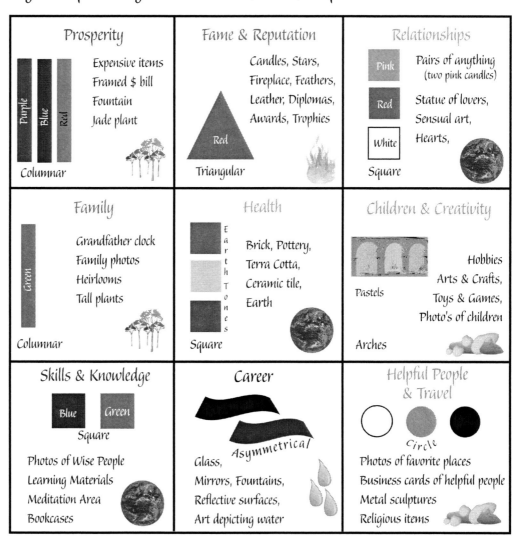

Prosperity	Fame & Reputation	Relationships
Purple Blue Red — *Columnar*	Red — *Triangular*	Pink, Red, White — *Square*
Expensive items, Framed $ bill, Fountain, Jade plant	Candles, Stars, Fireplace, Feathers, Leather, Diplomas, Awards, Trophies	Pairs of anything (two pink candles), Statue of lovers, Sensual art, Hearts,

Family	Health	Children & Creativity
Green — *Columnar*	Earth Tones — *Square*	Pastels — *Arches*
Grandfather clock, Family photos, Heirlooms, Tall plants	Brick, Pottery, Terra Cotta, Ceramic tile, Earth	Hobbies, Arts & Crafts, Toys & Games, Photo's of children

Skills & Knowledge	Career	Helpful People & Travel
Blue Green — *Square*	*Asymmetrical*	*Circle*
Photos of Wise People, Learning Materials, Meditation Area, Bookcases	Glass, Mirrors, Fountains, Reflective surfaces, Art depicting water	Photos of favorite places, Business cards of helpful people, Metal sculptures, Religious items

Applying the Bagua Map to your Floor Plan

Applying the Bagua Map to One Room

Prosperity	Fame & Reputation	Relationships
Family	Health	Children & Creativity
Skills & Knowledge	Career	Helpful People & Travel

Applying the Bagua Map to the Plan of your Property

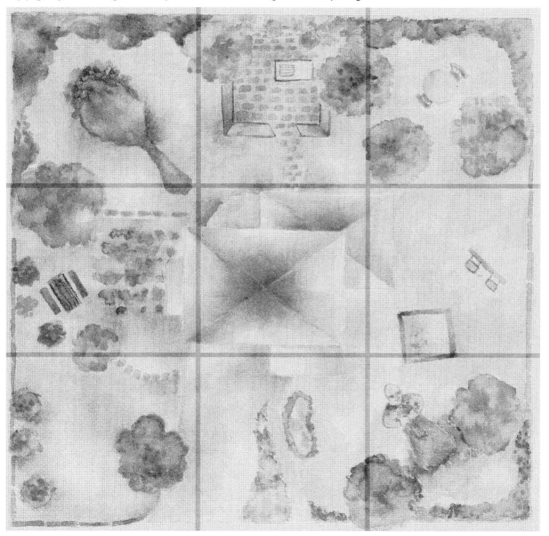

Applying the Bagua Map to Your Backyard

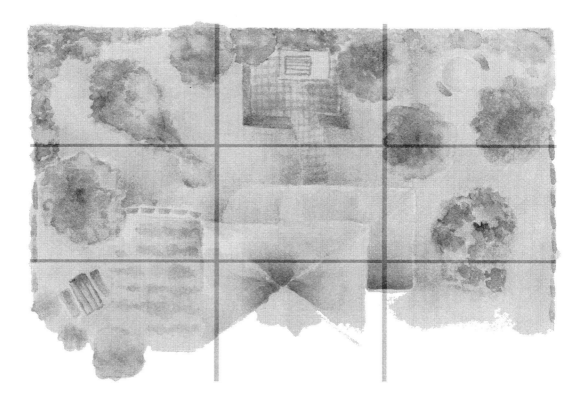

Not every house or piece of property is perfectly square or rectangular. Part of or an entire area may be "missing." Don't worry. If the floor plan of your home is missing an area, you can complete the missing area. For example, if your Prosperity area happens to be outside the house, you can complete ("anchor") that corner by adding the enhancements outdoors.

Anchor the missing areas with items such as these . . .

- Lamppost
- Flagpole
- Quartz crystal buried 5" to 6" deep pointing at the house
- Birdbath
- Gazing ball
- Flower bed
- Seating area
- Fountain (with water flowing toward the house
- . . . and then place a mirror on the inside wall of the missing area to symbolically bring that area inside the house

Prosperity Area Missing

Career Area Missing

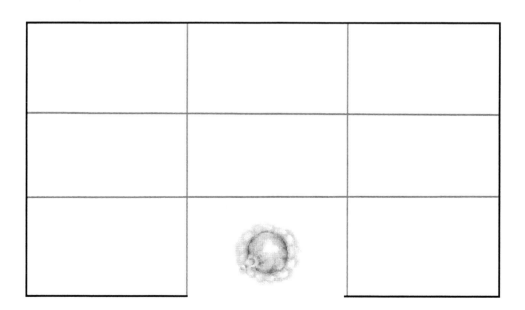

Skills & Knowledge and Career Areas Missing

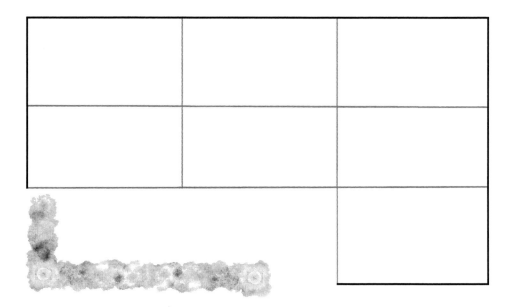

Each Bagua area is associated with a specific color and shape. If your kitchen is in the area associated with the Fire element but you don't want to paint your kitchen red, substitute items representing the Fire element such as candles, suns, or art depicting people or animals. Outside, good substitutions for red flowers might be animal statuary, pointy and conical items, or an outdoor fireplace or *chimenea*.

ELEMENT	COLOR SUBSTITUTION	SHAPE SUBSTITUTION
Water	Blue, black	Wavy, curvy, asymmetrical
Fire	Red	Pointy, conical
Metal	Gray, silver	Round, arched
Wood	Green	Columnar
Earth	Brown, yellow	Flat, square

Prosperity

This area correlates to the prosperity, abundance, and riches in your life—not merely your finances, but whatever you consider abundance to be. Enhance this area in your home or yard to feel you have more than enough.

Enhance with

- Purple, reds, and blues
- Wind chimes
- Crystals
- Piggy banks
- Valuable possessions
- Moving objects
- Art depicting desired possessions
- Things that remind you of wealth
- Flowing water feature or art depicting a waterfall
- Water fountains that pool water (to symbolize pooling wealth)
- Fish tank
- A group of three round-leaf plants that have purple blooms or coin-shaped leaves (African violets, jade)
- Three similar objects to represent continuity
- A bowl full of fresh fruit as a sign of abundance

Another tip to help boost your feelings of prosperity is to visit wealthy places to absorb the energy of prosperity. Wander through an expensive hotel lobby or have a drink at an expensive restaurant. Visit a luxury-car showroom or drive through an exclusive neighborhood. Do this often to create auspicious thoughts and new ideas.

Fame and Reputation

This area relates to your standing in the community and how others perceive you. It also has to do with your honesty, integrity, and direction toward a goal.

Enhance with:

- Red
- Pointy, conical, pyramid, triangle shapes (they point up, which is the direction you are going!)
- Candles, lighting, fireplaces
- Chile *ristra*
- High things: mountains, suns, moons, stars
- Art depicting people, animals, sunshine, fire
- Pets, wildlife, things made from animals (fur, bone, feathers, leather, wool)
- Diplomas, awards, prizes, and trophies
- Chandeliers

Relationships

This area relates to the status of your marriage or significant relationship. Enhance this area (even if it is not your bedroom) if you are having problems with your partner or are looking for a partner. Also enhance the opposite area on the Bagua Map (Skills and Knowledge) so you will have the ability to know if you are choosing the right person.

Enhance with

- Pink, white, and red
- Romantic, sensual art

- Photos of you and your partner
- Pairs of objects (two plants, two pillows, two candles)
- Art depicting couples
- Pink quartz crystal
- Fresh flowers
- Pink heart-shaped crystal in window
- Double happiness symbol

Family

This area concerns your immediate family as well as your relatives, ancestors and any genetic associations. Enhancing this area promotes family harmony.

Enhance with
- Green
- Columns, pedestals, poles, vertical stripes
- Columnar shapes, columns, posts
- Wooden furniture and frames, paneling
- Plants, flowers
- Art depicting trees, plants, and flowers
- Floral prints in drapes, linens, upholstery
- Family photos
- Family heirlooms
- Antiques

Health

Stability and emotional well-being are represented here.

Enhance with
- Earth tones, yellow
- Flat and square things
- Exercise equipment
- Brick, tile, adobe, terra-cotta, ceramics
- Art depicting earthy landscapes
- Healthy plants and freshly cut flowers
- Books about nutrition
- Representations of long life: tortoise, elephant

Children and Creativity

This area affects your creativity and communication and is connected to the well-being of your children. This is an excellent area in which to do hobbies, crafts, or artwork.

Enhance with

- Whites and pastels
- Circles and arches
- Metal things
- Crystals, gems
- Art made from metal or stone
- Art created by children
- Arts and crafts, hobbies

- Toys and games
- Whimsical things
- TVs, stereos, computers
- Children's photos
- Things from your childhood
- Pets' toys, food, or water
- A piece of artwork by an artist you admire
- Objects that have been made for you or made by you

Skills and Knowledge

This area relates to the inner spiritual areas of your life and is associated with grounding, knowledge, and wisdom.

Enhance with

- Greens and blues
- Books
- Study and educational materials
- Owls, elephants
- Meditation area
- Yoga
- Globe
- Pens, pencils, writing paper
- Good lighting
- Plants to represent growth
- A Buddha statue (symbolic of wisdom and knowledge, it stimulates the unconscious to become more receptive to learning)

Career

This area concerns your job and career success. Enhance this area if you would like to get a promotion, a better job or change careers.

Enhance with

Black and dark blues

- Wavy, curvy, asymmetrical, or undulating shapes
- A black welcome mat (if your front door is in this area)
- Fountains, aquarium, water features
- Art depicting waterfalls, pools, streams, rivers, oceans, or snow
- Glass, mirrors, crystal, reflective surfaces
- Black and white photos
- Symbols related to your career
- A healthy plant, representing the growth of your career

Helpful People and Travel

This area relates to synchronicity, being in the right place at the right time, networking, and lucky encounters. It is also associated with mentors and helpful people in your life (doctor, lawyer, and travel agent, for example). This area also relates to travel you do or desire to do.

Enhance with

- Grey, black, and white
- Round and oval shapes

- Metal objects
- Art or travel posters depicting places you would like to visit
- Religious or spiritual figures associated with your own beliefs—angels, buddhas, saints, gods, and goddesses
- Photos or inspirational sayings of mentors
- Eagles (representing you soaring to new places)
- Pictures of modes of travel (cars, planes, trains)

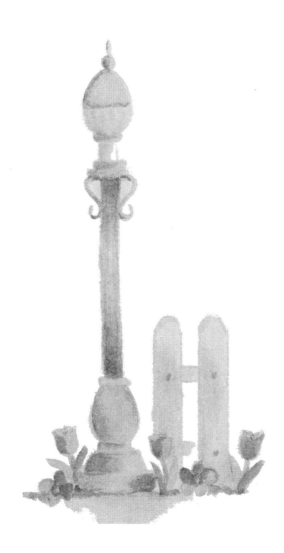

Cures in Feng Shui are conscious and subconscious motivators. Even if you are not consciously aware of it, the symbolic enhancements you place are creating the power of suggestion. By placing positive images and objects in our environment, we are activating mental energies that create positive thoughts.

Crystals

A popular object used in Feng Shui is the round-faceted crystal. Crystals balance Chi that is moving either too fast or too slow. They shift the energy of a space by attracting light and new energy. When sunlight hits a crystal, beams of colored light radiate, creating beautiful rainbows on your walls and activating Chi energy. The size of the crystal you choose depends on the amount of energy you are trying to transform. When you hang your crystal, think of the intention you want to manifest in your life.

When you get your crystals home, be sure to clean them. It's a good idea to clean them routinely to keep them at their best, because their capacity to enhance the energy around them is linked to their cleanliness. You can reactivate your crystals by cleaning them with cold water and sea salt and hanging them outside to be bathed in the light of the full moon.

Good places for crystals

- In the middle of a long hallway to disperse rushing energy.
- Between doors that are misaligned in a hallway.
- Between the front door and the window or door in the back of the house if you can see into your back yard when you enter your front door.
- Between your front door and stairs going up or down.
- In the Children and Creativity area of your home to increase creativity.

- Over your desk chair to enhance clearer thinking and better decision-making.
- Over your bed if you have a slanted ceiling.
- Over your bed to enhance inner growth, peace, and a deeper sleep.
- Over the head of your bed to enliven your sexual intimacy.
- Over your dining room table if you have a slanted ceiling.
- At a sharp corner of a wall or column.
- In the Prosperity area if you would like more wealth.
- Under a skylight.
- In the Skills and Knowledge area to enhance mental clarity.

Mirrors

Mirrors are one of the most frequently used cures for Feng Shui ailments. Mirrors can be used to create the illusion of space, to bring in light, to symbolically double energy (put one with your loose change), and to bring in beautiful views from outside.

Mirror tips

- If you have a body of water or other great view near your home, use a mirror inside so that you can also see the view in the mirror.
- Hang a mirror on the wall facing a missing area to symbolically dissolve the wall and make the missing area available.
- Don't use mirrored tiles—you don't want to see your image broken up.
  A dressing mirror should not cut off your feet or your head.
- Don't hang mirrors opposite your entrance door. All the energy that comes in will be reflected back out.
- And don't hang mirrors opposite each other—the Chi just bounces back and forth.

Water Features

The sound and motion of moving water activates Chi and creates a relaxed atmosphere. Moving water brings prosperity and good luck. The Chinese equate the flow of water to the flow of money, which is why so many Chinese businesses have aquariums or fountains on their premises.

If you have an outdoor water feature, make sure the water flows toward your house, symbolizing money flowing toward you instead of away from you. The same is true indoors—water should not flow out. If you have a water feature in your living room, be sure it is on the left side of the door looking out. The Chinese believe that if a water feature is placed on the right side, it will cause the man of the house to stray.

Water fountains, aquariums, and art depicting water are great enhancements for your Career and Prosperity areas.

Intention and Affirmation

What you think about, you bring about. When placing a Feng Shui cure, have a clear intention of what you want, visualize the desired result, speak your intention, and expect the result to happen. This allows you to mentally reinforce the changes you are making. Applying specific intention to cures creates extra energy. Each time you see a cure you have placed, it will trigger positive thoughts.

Affirmations are positive statements that stimulate our subconscious mind and create a shift in our thought process. If you send negative messages to your subconscious—"I'm so broke" or "I hate my life"—that is just what will manifest. You can change your life by reprogramming your subconscious mind and sending it positive messages. Your thoughts are powerful. Positive energy is attracted to positive energy.

When placing cures, phrase affirmations in the present tense.

Prosperity

- Wealth flows easily into my life.
- I have a constant flow of money.
- I have financial security.
- I have the money I need for what I desire.

Fame and Reputation

- I am respected by the people I work with.
- The people in my community support my accomplishments.
- I am respected for my skills and talents.
- I have a reputation for honesty and trustworthiness.
- I have integrity.

Health

- I am a healthy person.
- I eat healthy foods and exercise.
- I am full of vitality.

Family

- I enjoy wonderful relationships with my family.
- I have great relatives.
- My friends are an extension of my family.

Relationships

- Love always surrounds me.
- I attract love into my life.
- My partner and I have a mutually respectful relationship.

Children and Creativity

- My children are living their lives to their fullest potential.
- I express my creativity easily.
- My creative juices are constantly flowing.

Career

- My career is enjoyable and financially rewarding.
- I have my dream job.
- I attract lucrative career opportunities.

Skills and Knowledge

- I am a wise person.
- I know what to do in any situation.
- I am constantly learning.

Helpful People and Travel

- I am always in the right place at the right time.
- Synchronicities are constantly happening in my life.
- I attract helpful people to my life.
- I travel to places I enjoy as often as I like.

Bed placement

Good placement: *You can see the door to the room while lying in bed.*

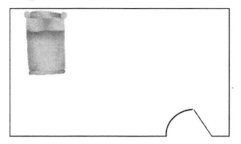

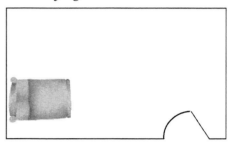

Less desirable placement:

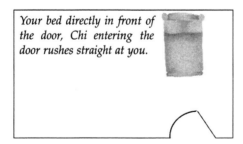

Your bed directly in front of the door, Chi entering the door rushes straight at you.

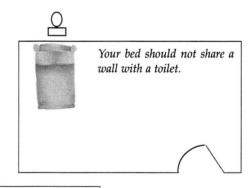

Your bed should not share a wall with a toilet.

Your bed should not be on the same wall as the door because you can't see who is entering the room. To cure this hang a mirror on the wall opposite the door.

Entrance to Your Home

If you have a straight path, add healthy plants along its edges to soften the straight lines. This encourages the Chi to slow down and meander more slowly toward your home. Chi races down straight paths with only the intention of getting to the other end.

Install easy-to-read house numbers, and make sure your address is clearly visible from the street. Include symbols of welcome at your front entrance—wind chimes, a fountain, pots of flowers, a bench, an attractive doormat, a freshly painted front door. The front door of your home is considered the "mouth of Chi," through which opportunities and energy enter your home. The front door sets the tone of your home. This is where people form their first impressions of you. We should treat ourselves like guests by providing a welcoming entrance. Be sure to use your front door each day, even if you usually enter your home through a different door.

Make sure your front door is always clear, unobstructed, well-lit, and sheltered from the elements. If it is stuck or it squeaks—or a pile of stuff prevents it from opening freely—the effect is often that opportunity is prevented from flowing toward you. This is also the case if the doorbell doesn't work.

Cover glass in your door or windows beside the door to give yourself an enhanced feeling of security. If you can see right out into your backyard from the front door,

Your Home's Location

T-Intersection. If your street ends at your house, energy is bombarding you. Cure the effects of rushing Chi by planting a tall hedge or building a fence across the front of the property. Hang a Bagua mirror over your front door and hang wind chimes at your front door to disperse oncoming energy.

Cul-de-Sacs. A cul-de-sac has no outlet for the energy flowing into it, so you are living in stuck energy all the time. Attract fresh energy to your house by adding a fountain in front, wind chimes, a flag, or wind sock.

Dead-End Streets. Dead-end streets get less energy than cul-de-sacs. Energy cannot flow through and is less active. How about a bird feeder and birdbath to add life to your yard?

place a small mirror on the window frame or the door and hang a crystal in the window. This will keep the energy in the house.

Inside Your Home

Living Room   Some people hardly ever step foot in their living rooms. Use your living room to entertain and as a place for the family to gather otherwise the chi in that unused room will become stagnant.

Tips for your living room

- You should be able to see your front door from wherever you are sitting.
- Don't overcrowd the room with too much furniture.
- Enable traffic to flow freely. You should be able to walk through the room without bumping into anything.
- Have good lighting. This room should be Yang.

Kitchen   According to Feng Shui, the kitchen is one of the most important rooms in the home. The kitchen symbolizes the wealth of the family, and its condition reveals a great deal about your financial situation. It is where the family's food is cooked, and the quality and quantity of food available in a home strongly reflects the family's prosperity, overall health, and well-being.

Tips for your kitchen

- Avoid having a kitchen island, as it attracts clutter.
- Be sure you can see the door to the room while you're standing at the stove. If you

can't, hang a mirror or something else with a reflective surface on the wall behind the stove so you can see who is coming into the room.

- Healthy plants purify the air in the kitchen.
- Minimize countertop clutter. Only keep items on your countertops that you use regularly and that do not get in the way.
- Go through your cupboards to clear out food you don't like or want, and donate it to a shelter or food bank.
- Open a window or use an overhead fan for ventilation.
- Keep your stove clean and in good working order.
- Keep knives and other sharp or pointed things in a drawer.
- Throw away broken or chipped dishes.
- Have good bright lighting.
- Clean out the refrigerator—and don't forget the top.
- Water faucet dripping, drain clogged? Get these repaired.

Dining Room These days, we often rush through our meals, not even sitting at a dining room table together. We eat in the kitchen, in our cars, or in front of the television. The fine art of dining has been designated as a special event. When you actually do eat in the dining room, create a pleasant and serene environment.

Tips for your dining room

- Create a soothing atmosphere that is conducive to conversation.
- Make sure that your dining room furniture is comfortable.
- Repair or replace unsafe chairs.
- Select art that is relaxing.
- Round tables are preferred over square or rectangular shapes with sharp edges.

- Eat in your dining room occasionally to keep the energy flowing.
- Don't watch television or read the newspaper during meals.
- Seat the head of household facing the door to the room.
- Since circles symbolize harmony, having a circular rug under the table brings people together.
- Ensure the chairs don't obstruct doorways.
- Install a dimmer switch to change the atmosphere for different occasions.
- Don't have a clock in the dining room—it makes people feel rushed.

Bedrooms In Feng Shui, the belief is that the more time spent in a room, the more influence that room has on one's life. We spend about one-third of our lives sleeping. Make your bedroom beautiful and comfortable and a place to promote rest and relaxation. Locate bedrooms in the back of the house where it is quieter and away from street noise. Use your bedroom as a sanctuary, a place to sleep and be romantic. Any other activities belong in another room.

Water beds do not provide suitable support. Water is a fluid element and takes the shape of its surroundings. Water beds also have a heating element that produces magnetic fields and can disrupt sleep. A conventional bed with a solid frame and good mattress is preferred. Have a solid headboard, which symbolizes support. Be able to access both sides of the bed.

Keep the energy Yin to create a restful, relaxing, serene atmosphere. Use warm flesh-toned colors. Cool colors make the room less cozy. Use soft lighting—use pink light bulbs. If you keep the lights low in your bedroom, you won't be tempted to work and read there.

Place your bed in a commanding position so you can see the door to the room without having to reposition yourself. This removes the possibility of being startled by someone entering the room and being unconsciously stressed by wondering if someone is peeking in on you. Don't place the bed under exposed beams, especially if the beam divides a couple. Don't place your bed under a slanted ceiling. The ceiling directs energy down toward you and may give you the feeling of being oppressed.

Don't sleep with your feet pointing directly out the door. This is referred to by the Chinese as the "death position" as it suggests the position of a coffin before it leaves a home. Also, Chi rushing from the door directly to the bed is too powerful.

A bathroom that is attached to the bedroom should be screened or its door kept closed. Positioning your bed back-to-back on a common wall with a toilet is bad, because the flushing sucks positive energy. Don't place your bed under a window. According to Feng Shui principles, this causes feelings of vulnerability.

Don't place your bed opposite a mirror. Mirrors may contribute to poor sleep as they bounce energy back and forth. Also, it may be disturbing to wake up in the middle of the night and see your reflection. Since you want peaceful energy in the bedroom, try covering the mirrors (especially closet doors with full-length mirrors) with a curtain at night to see if it makes a difference.

Keep electrical items (TVs and computers) out of the bedroom. Don't sleep under an electric blanket. The electricity disturbs sleep and can deplete the immune system. Avoid synthetic fabrics on your bed and in bedroom carpeting. They increase static electricity. Use natural materials such as cotton, flannel, or silk for sheets, blankets, and bed and floor coverings.

Single Person's Bedroom

If you are looking for a romantic partner, enhance your bedroom with visual affirmations supporting your desire.

- Have equal-sized bed tables on either side of the bed.
- Make sure there is access to the bed from both sides.
- Leave some room in the closet for your new partner's clothes.
- Use art portraying couples, not pictures of a person alone.
- Bedroom décor should appeal to both partners. Try to strike a balance between leather and lace. Women, don't make your bedroom too "girly" by covering your bed with dolls or stuffed animals. Men, display your hunting trophies in your office.
- Remove family pictures.

Couple's Bedroom

The bedroom is one of the most important rooms in a home. An auspicious bedroom brings harmony to the family. The ambience in this room should be restful to ensure sound sleep. The bedroom must be clean and free of clutter so the energy won't become stagnant. The bedroom should be your sanctuary where you are able to shut out the world. Both partners should like the décor.

- Use romantic or sensual art. Remove any negative imagery, including representations of solitude or loneliness.
- Display pairs of anything (hearts, candles, pillows, a pair of doves as a symbol of peace and harmony, or a pair of swans—they mate for life).

- Remove old-relationship energy by getting rid of anything that reminds you of past failed relationships (especially your mattress).
- Display pictures of you as a couple. Remove all photos of friends and relatives. It's hard to be intimate if you feel like your family and friends are watching.
- Use your bedroom as a bedroom—no computers or workout equipment.
- If you have a fireplace in your bedroom, add a healthy plant or art depicting water to balance out all the fire energy.
- If you have an attached bathroom, always keep the door closed.
- Open windows often to allow fresh energy in (especially if you use air conditioning).
- Burning two red candles will create passion.
- Burning two pink candles will create affection.
- Don't use the area under the bed for storage. Remember, Chi cannot flow through clutter.
- Make sure the bed has access from both sides and that bed tables are of equal size.
- Luxurious natural-fiber fabrics stimulate your sense of touch.
- Pink sheets enhance feelings of love and romance.
- Fabrics with circles symbolize unity and wholeness.
- Fabrics with triangles encourage action and excitement.
- Rose quartz brings love and luck.

If you have a king-size bed with two separate box springs, place a red sheet over them to symbolically bring them together. Red can increase romance and passion, but also be aware that but too much red can cause friction and arguments. Monitor this cure and make adjustments if necessary.

Teenager's Bedroom

Teens want more of place to hang out rather than a bedroom. They love black. Let them have some. They also love candles. Just make sure the candle holders are safe. Open the windows often to allow in fresh energy. Explain to the kids that clearing out their closet will create a space for new clothes.

Go with the flow and stay out of their rooms. Their clutter will not affect the overall energy of the house. If they know you aren't going through their things behind their backs, they are much more likely to return that trust and confide in you.

Child's Bedroom

Your child's room should have lots of natural light. Paint the walls in soothing colors rather than primary colors. Bright colors may excite and overstimulate, while dark colors may be draining or depressing. Rose quartz disperses fears. Use vertical stripes to represent a feeling of growth. Keep pictures current so kids don't get "stuck" being a baby. Include family photos for a feeling of comfort.

Make sure kids can see the door from their bed. They should not be able to see themselves in a mirror while in bed because it may startle them to wake up in the middle of the night and see their reflection.   If they have a desk in the room, position it so they can see the door to the room while working.

Keep clutter from under the bed, and don't have shelves over the bed. Don't use bunk beds—they are not a favorite in Feng Shui for a few reasons. Since bunk beds are usually placed against a wall, you are giving your child only one option, only one way out. The child in the bottom bunk may feel subconsciously threatened by the fact that the top bunk may fall on him. The top occupant may feel claustrophobic with the ceiling so close to his head, as well as nervous about falling out of the bed.

Have a place for everything. Contribute toys the kids have outgrown to charity. Encourage your kids to pick things up off the floor in their rooms at the end of the day to leave room for angels to dance at night.

Nursery

To get your nursery ready for the baby, clear the current energy of the room. You can do this by simply leaving the windows open on a sunny day to let in fresh air. If you are using a hand-me-down crib, realize that it possesses the energy of its previous occupant. Buy a new mattress, and clean the crib well.

Use soft, soothing pastel colors and simple designs to create a restful environment. Primary colors tend to overstimulate.

Locate the crib against a wall, not under a window or in direct line with the main entrance into the bedroom. Babies intuitively move themselves so that the tops of their heads are pointing toward their most comfortable direction. If you notice that your baby changes its sleeping position, turn the crib to match it.

Don't hang mobiles over your baby's head. Hang them in a corner or over the changing table.

Hang a crystal in the window to create sparkling energy. Place a guardian angel to protect your child in the Helpful People area of the room.

Spend time with the baby in the nursery so it will associate the space with comfort and contentment.

Guest Bedroom

If your guest bedroom is in the front of the house, your guests won't overstay their welcome. If it is the back of the house, they may be there for awhile. If you have a photograph of them with you enjoying a previous visit, place it in their room. It will make them feel like part of the family.

Bedroom over a Garage

Subconsciously, we need to feel protected and safe in order to deeply rest. The person sleeping over the garage may be affected by either the emptiness or the clutter below. Because the garage is where cars go in and out, the energy is always moving. There may be paint, gasoline and other toxic materials in your garage, not to mention the exhaust fumes. Be sure there is no air traveling from the garage to the bedroom through your ventilation system.

You can reflect away the energy in the garage by placing a mirror face-down on the floor under the bed or place an additional layer of carpet to further insulate the occupant from the garage energy.

Bathroom   The bathroom's purpose is to dispose of used water and human waste through the drains of the sink, toilet, bathtub, and shower. Always keep the bathroom door closed, and always keep the toilet lid down when not in use. Where the eye goes the Chi flows.

Balance all the water energy by decorating with fiery colors or earth tones. Use the wood (green accessories and plants) and earth element to soak up the water rather than adding more water (for example, fish, seashells, nautical themes).

Tips for your bathroom

- Keep countertops clutter free.
- Add Yang energy with candles.
- Prevent the Chi from escaping down the drains by keeping them closed.
- Toilets, sinks, and showers pull energy down. Lift energy by hanging a crystal above them.
- Fix dripping faucets.
- Keep safety in mind and use non-slip surfaces.
- If you have a window in your bathroom, let fresh air in daily.
- Mirrors can visually enlarge a small room; just don't use mirrored tiles that break up your image.
- Hang artwork above the toilet to take your attention away from the toilet.

Home Office Since energy enters your home through the front door, the best place for your home office is in the front of the house to take advantage of that flow of energy. If you're in the back, it's more difficult to receive that energy. Having your office in the front of your home will also be easier if you will be meeting with clients in your home.

It is preferable to be on the entry level or above as opposed to a level below the main floor of the house. It's difficult for energy to move down into the basement. If your home office is located in the basement, paint the walls and ceilings a bright white and use bright lighting. Install a fan to get the energy moving.

If you don't have a view outside from your office chair, brighten the room with yellow paint, bright lights, and pictures of the outdoors. Your ceiling should be painted a light color—a dark color will make you feel as if there's a dark cloud hanging over your head while you work.

Always sit facing the door to give yourself a feeling of control. Having your back to the door creates feelings of insecurity and vulnerability and will cause you to be jumpy, easily startled, and distracted because you never know who's behind you or you'll feel like you're being stabbed in the back. If you absolutely have to sit with your back to the door, hang a mirror in front of you or angled above your desk so that you can see anyone walking into the room.

Clutter tip

If there is something on your desk that you haven't touched in a month, file it away.

Don't place your desk so that your back is against a full wall of windows. This position may make you feel as though nothing solid is backing you up. Position your desk facing into the room rather than facing a wall. Don't put it where you feel cramped and confined, where your field of vision is limited, or where there is a passageway behind you.

Clutter in your home office affects your prosperity, productivity, energy, creativity, and work with clients. Eliminating the clutter will make room for something new and desirable to enter. Display items that signify wealth. Hang positive art about your business success. Hang diplomas and awards in your Fame area.

Sit on a comfortable chair. Make sure your lighting is adequate. Don't have shelves above your head. Activate Chi by hanging a crystal in the window. Have a water fountain in your Career area. The sound of the water will reduce stress.

Arrange the top of your desk using the Bagua Map. The Prosperity area or upper left corner is the most important part of your home office or desk. Place your calculator or a healthy plant in this area to enrich your business. A red object such as red flowers placed in the upper left corner can bring financial success-placed in the back center portion of your office or desk can bring fame. Display a pyramid on your desk. The upward-pointing triangle signifies growth. If it is red, it will stimulate activity.

Select an auspicious screen saver for your computer. Declutter your computer. Purge e-mail files occasionally.

Desk Bagua

Jade plant in purple pot, calculator	Your business cards, a lamp, awards	Photo of your partner, a pair of anything
Family photo in wooden frame		Children's photos in silver frame, colored markers
Reference materials, Current projects	Black desk blotter	Business cards of helpful people, telephone, trip photos

Architectural Features

Windows Windows are important for bringing in the natural energy from the sun. Ideally they should all open fully and outward. Too many windows can create excessive Yang energy as they blast the house with Chi, while too few windows are Yin. Make sure you have a pleasant view from all of your windows. If you keep your curtains closed during the day, chances are that you will feel depressed and vulnerable. The aim is to see out as much as possible.

Hallways Chi rushes quickly down long hallways. To slow it down, hang a crystal in the hallway. Placing a few small area rugs will have the same effect.

Stairways If there is a staircase in a direct line with your front door, hang a crystal or a wind chime halfway between the door and the stairs to stop the Chi from rushing down the stairs and right out the door. Hang pictures in a horizontal line level instead of sloping down the stairs. The horizontal line will slow the Chi.

Spiral Staircases Spiral staircases act as a "drill" through your home. Chi flows right through the open treads and doesn't make it upstairs. To help cure the spiral, place a large plant at the base underneath the stairs, hang a crystal or wind chime at the top of the stairs, or wrap a silk vine or garland around the banister.

Slanted Ceilings Slanted ceilings are oppressive. When you spend a lot of time in a space where the ceiling slants down toward you, you may feel like the Chi is pressing down on you and disturbing your personal energy. Sleeping or working under a slanted ceiling depresses your energy, interfering with your sleep at night and your creativity during the day.

To help cure these rooms, mirrors, lights, and paint color may help create the illusion of lifting the slope. Place small mirrors in the corners of the room or on top of a piece of furniture to lift the ceiling back up. Hang a faceted crystal ball to disperse this negative energy.

Beams Beams can be oppressive, suppressing the Chi of the people living beneath them, especially in a bedroom. It is said that a beam running along the length of the bed symbolically splits the couple. If you have a beam in your bedroom, avoid placing the bed directly underneath it. Also, cure this situation by painting the beam a light color or the color of the ceiling. Use uplighting in the room.

Skylights Adding a skylight to your home is like performing surgery on your roof. As you know, some surgeries go well, while others don't. Although skylights are great for letting in additional light, prevent Chi from leaking out through the roof by hanging a crystal under your skylight. If sleeping under the skylight disturbs your sleep, move your bed or cover the skylight at night.

Garage In Feng Shui, an attached garage is considered part of the house. If you enter your house from the garage, the condition of the garage affects you each day. What do you see when you first drive in? Hang a favorite print on the wall opposite the entrance to lift your energy each time you drive in. Keep your garage orderly and uncluttered. Arriving home to a messy garage and having to trip over things in order to get into the house will do nothing to improve your mood.

Attic and Basement Your attic symbolizes your mind and spiritual life. A cluttered attic creates a feeling of being under pressure. It is hard to feel optimistic about the future when there's so much stuff up there hanging over your head. Clearing the clutter will clarify your thinking. Your basement represents your subconscious. De-cluttering this area helps you clear out unresolved issues. Think about what is in your attic and basement:—old love letters, photographs, baby clothes, extra stuff, unfinished projects. There are probably things in these spaces you haven't used in years that perhaps someone else could use.

Color Color strongly affects our moods and can also appear to change the size, shape, and energy of a room. It can brighten a room and add excitement and stimulation. Just one gallon of paint can dramatically change a room. Bright colors enliven; dark colors create peace.

> **Green** is refreshing, relaxing, soothing, and calming. It makes us feel alive. It is associated with healing, wisdom, growth, creativity, fertility, harmony, balance, and tranquility.

> **Red** is a dramatic color that captures the attention. It is passionate, stimulating, empowering, and activating and has associations with joy, love, strength, happiness, and confidence. Red is also an aggressive color. It's a good choice for anyone making

deals or selling. The reason you see so much red in Chinese restaurants is because the Chinese believe red brings forth good business. Feng Shui uses red ribbon to hang crystals and adds red to many of the enhancements to activate them.

Yellow creates feelings of warmth, safety, and stability. It represents long life and immortality, and it increases energy. Yellow enhances optimism, clear thinking, intuition, and insight. It is associated with authority and communication.

White is associated with purity, truth, harmony, and trustworthiness. It energizes, unifies, and improves concentration and clear thinking. It brings life to all other colors.

Black is associated with peacefulness. Black is dramatic and powerful. It increases communication and mental activity, and encourages independence. It has associations with mystery and the unknown.

Purple is a soothing color that enhances calm and thoughtfulness. It represents spirituality, creates mystery, and draws out intuition. It reinforces power and strength and is associated with dignity and wisdom.

Pink is a soothing color and is associated with love and romance and produces feelings of sociability and affection. It supports love, self-awareness, and spiritual contentment.

Orange stimulates the appetite, conversation, charity, and collaboration. It is the color of hope, enthusiasm, confidence, and organization.

Blue produces relaxed, tranquil feelings and peaceful moods; it harmonizes, refreshes, and cools. Blue builds self-esteem.

Family Photographs. Keep the photos you display in your home current. If a teenager walks into the house each day and sees a picture of himself as a baby, he may subconsciously get stuck in the past—seeing himself as, and acting like, a baby.

Make sure no one is left out of family photos. Display only photos that include the whole family. The ones taken before the last child was born should be put away in an album. A relaxed, happy photograph of the family is best. Staged professional photographs create a feeling of stiffness that will be reinforced every time you look at that photo.

Artwork. The images we surround ourselves with exert a powerful subconscious influence on our thoughts and emotions. Before you hang artwork, consider whether its message will help or harm your life.

For example, where people have busy, angular, or aggressive images in their homes, they complain of stress, arguments, or poor communication. Someone surrounded by imagery that is predominantly calm and sedate or that displays strong earth energy may say they feel stuck. Someone who tends to collect pictures of solitary people might be happily single. If you are looking for a relationship, though, display art portraying couples.

The message of your artwork is as important as its visual appeal. Decide if their messages are appropriate for the Bagua areas in which you place them.

Live Plants and Flowers. The insides of our homes are as much as ten times more polluted than our outdoor environment—and we spend about 90 percent of our time inside buildings. We are surrounded by synthetics—in carpeting, draperies, furniture held together with glues and resins . . . not to mention the large number of electrical devices in our lives. We work in hermetically sealed buildings with no ventilation where we are exposed to other human beings and their accompanying germs.

Fresh air from outdoors helps to control indoor air pollution. Also, we can add some oxygen and beauty to our indoor environments by using house plants, which have the ability to remove formaldehyde and other chemicals from the air. (Yes, formaldehyde—it's present in such common items as garbage bags, paper towels, and tissues.) House plants also release chemicals that can suppress the presence of mold spores and bacteria by up to 50 percent. And they can diffuse electrical currents that emanate from electronic equipment.

Healthy, vibrant plants are an easy solution to many Feng Shui problems. They can balance the Chi of a room, increase its oxygen content, and clean pollutants from the air. Avoid plants with sharp, pointy leaves such as cactus and spider plants. Sick plants give off negative energy. Throw away dead or dying plants and replace them with healthy ones.

The wood energy of plants represents new beginnings and growth. It balances the earth element, which may be represented in the square shapes of our houses, rooms, and furniture. Healthy plants and flowers are a great way to activate energy in stagnant corners and achieve a positive flow of Chi.

To attract wealth, use plants with round, coin-shaped leaves or a money tree. Tall, spiky plants belong in the Fame area. Put a money tree in your Prosperity area. And as for Lucky Bamboo—just add water, no sunlight necessary. Anyone with a black thumb can grow it!

Dried, Silk, and Artificial Flowers. Because they are a physical manifestation of a life that is no longer vital, dried flowers are symbolically associated with death. Nevertheless, you can associate dried flowers with positive events and activities (prom night, weddings, anniversaries). Seasonal wreaths are often designed exclusively with dried flowers. If you don't have a green thumb and can't seem to keep plants healthy and alive, feel free to use artificial plants and silk or dried flowers. It is better than having an unhealthy plant, which depletes Chi.

Dried flowers do have a life span, however. Replace them when their attractiveness has faded. Also, keep silk and other artificial flowers clean.

Pets. Pets significantly improve the quality of our lives. They are also great Chi generators. They circulate energy with their every move. Animals (especially cats) usually gravitate to the lowest energy in an environment, thus protecting their owners from negative electromagnetic fields of energy. Notice how your cat always seems to pick the most uncomfortable place to lie down?

Before you adopt a pet, be sure you have the time, money, and lifestyle to provide it with a healthy, happy life. A neglected pet sends out negative energy. If you are allergic to animals and can't have a pet, display pictures of pets for symbolic energy.

Use these simple Feng Shui tips to create a calm, relaxing, comfortable atmosphere for your entertaining.

Clean up your front entrance to make arriving guests feel welcome.

Set the mood and pamper your guests. While entertaining, when it comes to lighting, less is more. Candles create a warm atmosphere. Use short candles, as long ones tend to create barriers. Make sure they are unscented so the aromas of your delicious dinner can be appreciated. Use your fine china to exude an aura of wealth and prosperity. Use fresh flowers to bring in new energy. Centerpieces should be low enough that people can see each other over them.

A red tablecloth adds warmth, invites conversation, and stimulates the appetite. Avoid using "busy" tablecloths, as they are a distraction. Also, black or white table-cloths are not conducive to eating. To create a Yin atmosphere for a quiet, romantic dinner, play soft music and dim the lights, and use floral or soft-colored napkins. A red or pink tablecloth encourages romance. To create a Yang atmosphere for a party with lots of energy and excitement, use bright colors (add some red), expensive china and silverware, candles, spicy foods, and lively music.

Round tables are the best for conversation. Banish clocks from the dining room so your guests won't feel rushed (or wonder if the football game has started yet). Leave room for guests to get in and out of their chairs. The most important guest should sit in the "power position" with a full view of the entrance to the room. Also, be aware that people seated near the door become unsettled from the movement behind them and tend to leave first.

After your party is over, do a space clearing to reclaim your space.

Remember, it is *not* necessary to spend the holidays with your relatives. If you dread the holidays for this reason, make a healthy choice and spend time with people who lift your energy rather than drain it!

Traveling (Feng Shui Away From Home)

If you travel a lot, you're likely to end up in hotel rooms that just don't feel right. You can shift the energy of an uncomfortable room to create a restful haven for yourself by making a Feng Shui travel kit and keeping it in your suitcase.

> Feng Shui Travel Kit
> Bagua mirror
> Three small mirrors and tack gum for hanging them
> Suction cup with hook
> A scented candle or incense
> A round-faceted crystal
> A photo of your family, friends, or pets

When you arrive, your first move should be to have some fresh flowers delivered to your room. Burn the incense or a scented candle to clear the room of energy from the previous occupants. The round-faceted crystal can be hung in the window to catch rainbows of light. Display the favorite photograph you brought.

If your view is less than desirable, place a bagua mirror in the window, facing out, to deflect the unattractive or undesirable energy away from you. You can also adhere a mirror to the outside of a bathroom door if the door is in line with your bed.

If you cannot see the door to your room while you are lying in bed, position a mirror so that you'll see the entryway in its reflection. This eliminates any feeling of vulnerability.

Disconnect

What ever happened to that black phone in Aunt Bea's kitchen—and the slower lifestyle that went with it? Fifty years ago, that was our only choice in phones. But times have changed. Soon we could have a phone in the kitchen, on the wall, on a table, in the bedroom, in any style or color. Every teenage girl had to have a pink Princess phone. Today we even have phones in the bathroom. We have portable phones, pagers, cell phones . . . everyone in the family has their own phone and their own phone number.

How did we manage to survive before answering machines or call waiting or caller ID? Yes, there are emergencies—but will the world come to an end if we disconnect from our phones for a while?

Simplify your life. Consider not taking your cell phone:

- In the car
- On a plane
- To the grocery store
- On a walk alone or with your dog
- On your bike
- To the golf course
- To the beach
- On vacation
- Out in the yard
- To the movies
- To a waiting room

Enjoy the activities you are participating in. That's why you are doing them, isn't it? (The exception here is grocery shopping.) Yes, please try simplifying your life!

Take a Media Fast

Don't watch the news every night. When is the last time you felt great after watching the news? The news is mostly *bad* news. And reading the newspaper is not exactly the best way to start your day. Everything you read about murder, rape, robbery, and war first thing in the morning will be stuck in your subconscious all day long. If something really important happens in the world that you absolutely need to know about, believe me, you will hear about it in another way.

Use That Mute Button

We should all thank the person who invented the mute button on the television remote control. Use it! We'll get along just fine if we miss the moronic car salesman . . . the commercials about the drastic side effects of the latest miracle drug . . .the latest and greatest time-saving microwaveable product that contains mostly preservatives and very little worth eating . . .

Be Organized

Energy and time. We need lots of both these days. If you spend any time at all looking for your car keys, you are wasting energy. Designate a place for your keys, and keep them there all the time. If you can't find anything to wear in your stuffed closet, go through it and give away things you don't wear. Studies show that you only wear 20 percent of your clothes 80 percent of the time. Every little bit of energy you can save cuts down on stress, and you can use that energy for something productive.

Use the Internet

For shopping. To save time and to eliminate the hassles of traveling to malls—and the crowds once you get there—buy online. Shopping for clothing online may not work, but you can certainly use the Internet for things you're sure about. For instance, buy your books at Amazon.com or Barnes and Noble.com. Their prices are lower than prices in stores, and often you can get free shipping. Gift certificates are also a great online purchase.

For banking. You can cut three-fourths of the time you spend paying bills (not to mention the cost of the stamps) by using online banking. This also cuts down on clutter. Simply open your bills when you receive them and throw away *everything* except the actual bill. You won't need the return envelope, you won't need to write checks, and you won't need to lick stamps.

For information. If you need information from a business, check its Web site before telephoning. You may get your answer without having to negotiate an automated number-punching system. Don't you hate it when the first thing you are asked to punch in is your account number—and when you finally *do* get a person, the first thing they ask you for is your account number? #@$%(*!?!! Using a Web site will also save you time by keeping you from becoming involved in a conversation with a live person.

You can find practically everything on the Internet today. You can find phone numbers and zip codes, buy stamps, get driving directions and maps, make airline and hotel reservations, buy insurance, get tickets to sporting events and concerts, reserve a tee time at the golf course, subscribe to magazines, read newspapers, check movie listings, and pay bills.

Treat your yard as an extension of your home - an outdoor room. Feng Shui principles can be applied to your outdoor space according to your own style. It does not mean you will end up with an Asian-style garden. Create your own personal paradise, a peaceful place to relax in tranquil surroundings. Add beautiful colors and fragrant smells to give yourself a welcoming feeling when you arrive home each day. Plant a cutting garden to have your own supply of fresh flowers to enjoy inside your home. Invite movement, life and energy by adding wind chimes or a bird feeder, and plant an organic vegetable garden for pesticide-free produce.

When we apply Feng Shui principles to our outdoor space, we should keep the following things in mind:

Remove clutter to free up stagnant energy. In the garden, clutter can be anything from a pile of broken flowerpots to plants that are planted in the wrong place or plants you don't really like.

Keep your garden maintained by weeding and deadheading, removing debris, and pruning dead branches. If something is broken, it is best to repair it immediately before it gets worse. Squeaking gates, a broken hinge on a shed door, a burned-out bulb on an outside light—dealing with these things takes just moments, whereas if you ignore them it will nag at you indefinitely.

Create a series of outdoor rooms to expand your indoor living space. You can have a barbecue area for cooking, a garden patch where you grow organic vegetables, and a seating area where you can unwind and entertain.

Keep your trash cans out of sight. And remember, you can't hide from Feng Shui. Feng Shui applies in your garage and in your shed, so you need to keep these uncluttered as well.

Threshold

Create a threshold to make a smooth transition from the public's view to your private space. The approaching path should invite the visitor to explore and discover. The threshold should be wide enough to allow the visitor to slow for a moment and take in the view. This is a good place for some kind of "greeter" (like a garden sculpture, a welcome sign, or a pot of flowers).

Focal Point

Create a focal point in your garden that draws the attention. This could be a flower bed, a fountain, a gazebo, or a garden statue.

Boundaries

The ancient Chinese Feng Shui practitioners found that the ideal location for a home was with a mountain at the back and trees on the sides, creating an armchair effect. As you design your garden room, you can create that sense of defined space; a fence, trees, or tall shrubs can become your mountain, and bushes and flowers planted at either side will help to give you a sense of privacy from your neighbors.

Yard with fence in back and on sides

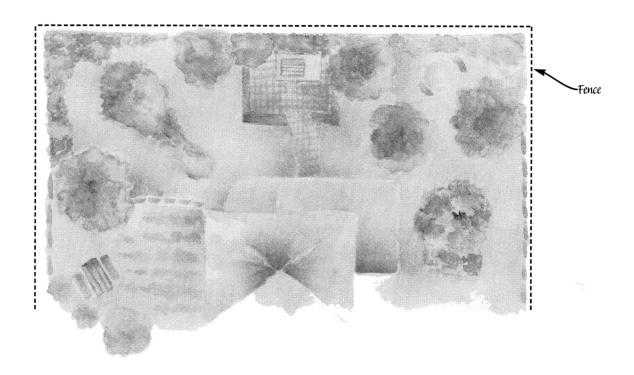

Fence

Defined Borders

Make clear boundaries for each area of activity and purpose (for your dog run, your vegetable garden, or where your kids play) to give the suggestion of different rooms. You can use all kinds of things as borders: bricks, stepping stones, stucco walls, a row of potted plants, hedges, arbors, or fences.

Pathways

You can use pathways to create an element of mystery that invites exploration. Pathways should be curved so that Chi can flow like a meandering stream. Make your pathway wide enough for two people to walk side by side. Invite your visitors to slow down and enjoy what they discover along the way.

Where paths meet, enlarge the junction. This gives the visitor space to pause and consider which way to go next. The junction itself can become a point of interest by placing a piece of garden statuary there.

Unnatural straight paths draw your attention to the end and speed the flow of Chi. Since Chi chooses the path of least resistance, it will race right out of your yard. If you have a straight path and cannot change it, plant flowers along the straight edges so that they overflow their beds a little, creating the illusion of a curve.

Balance

In the garden, we want to maintain a balance. Nothing should dominate. Everything should blend in harmoniously. We can achieve balance by mixing items that are rough and smooth, soft and hard, light and dark, and high and low. A balance of sunny and shady areas is ideal—and try to balance open, bright areas with sheltered retreats. When choosing plants, use a variety of sizes, shapes, and colors.

Incorporating the Five Elements in the Garden

Before you make any Feng Shui enhancements in your garden, you will be starting out with an abundance of earth. Earth is the actual soil and anything made from adobe, stucco, brick, terra-cotta, and pottery. However, to create the perfect outdoor environment, it's important to balance the five elements—wood, fire, water, metal, and earth.

If you already have trees and shrubs planted, the wood element is included. Any plant material you add is a wood element. To add the water element, consider a pond, fountain, or birdbath. If you install a pond with a waterfall, remember to have the water flowing toward your home, as a symbol of money flowing toward you. Metal can be added in the form of anything that is taken from the earth—rocks, stones, concrete, steel, marble, granite, and flagstone. The element of fire can be represented by your barbecue, a *chimenea*, torches, or lanterns.

Remember that you can substitute the characteristic shapes and associated colors for the actual elements. Red flowers or pointy-shaped plants can be substituted for a barbecue; arches and circles or silver foliage can be substituted for rocks and stones; and water can be represented by dark blue flowers and undulating shapes.

Landscaping with the Five Elements

WOOD	Plants, wooden decks, fencing, furniture, columnar shapes, greens
FIRE	Lighting, barbecues, pets, animal statuary, conical shapes, reds
EARTH	Brick, tile, adobe, terra-cotta, squares and rectangles, yellows, earth tones
METAL	Rocks, stones, concrete, flagstone, circular and oval shapes, whites, pastels
WATER	All water features, glass, crystals, asymmetrical shapes, black, dark blue

*E*nhancements in Feng Shui are conscious and subconscious motivators. Even if you are not consciously aware of it, the symbolic enhancements you place have the power of suggestion.

Prosperity

This area correlates to the prosperity, abundance and riches in your life, not only your finances but whatever you consider abundance to be.

Enhance with

- Purple, reds, and blues
- Wind chimes
- Moving objects—wind socks, whirligigs, flags
- Pond with waterfall flowing toward the house
- Water fountains that pool water (to symbolize pooling wealth)
- Fish, frogs
- Three similar plants to represent continuity
- Compost pile (nature's prosperity)
- Showy plants

Fame and Reputation

This area relates to how you are perceived by others and your standing in the community. It also has to do with your honesty and integrity and direction toward a goal.

Enhance with

- Red

- Pointy, conical, pyramid, triangle shapes. (They point up, which is the direction you are going!)
- Candles, lighting, torches, lanterns
- Barbecue
- Fireplaces
- *Chimenea*
- Chile *ristra*
- Suns, moons, stars
- Doghouse
- Wildlife
- Bird feeders and bird houses
- Animals and people statuary

Relationships

This area relates to the status of your marriage or significant relationship or, when enhanced, improves your chances of finding a partner. Enhance this area if you are having problems with your partner or looking for a new one. Also, enhance the opposite area (Skills and Knowledge) so you will have the ability to know if you are choosing the right person.

Enhance with

- Pink, white, and red flowers
- Table for two
- Bench for two
- Pairs of potted plants

- Statue of lovers
- Pairs of cranes, ducks, dolphins, doves
- Barbecue
- Fireplaces
- *Chimenea*
- Chile *ristra*
- Suns, moons, stars
- Doghouse
- Wildlife
- Bird feeders and bird houses
- Animals and people statuary

Family

This area concerns your immediate family, as well as your relatives and ancestors. Enhancing this area promotes family harmony.

Enhance with

- Green
- Columnar shapes, columns, posts, pedestals
- Wooden furniture
- Herb garden
- Picnic table
- Floral prints on patio furniture
- Antique garden implements

Health

Stability and overall well-being are represented here.

Enhance with

- Earth tones, yellow
- Flat and square things
- Brick
- Tile
- Adobe
- Terra-cotta
- Ceramics
- Stucco
- Representations of long life: tortoise, elephant

Children and Creativity

This area affects your creativity and communication and is connected to the well-being of your children.

Enhance with

- Whites and pastels
- Flagstone, granite, concrete
- Stones and rocks
- Circles and arches
- Metal objects

- Gazing balls
- Shiny objects
- Art made from metal or stone
- Swing set
- Whimsical things
- Pets' toys, food, or water
- A piece of artwork by an artist you admire
- Objects that have been made for you or made by you

Skills and Knowledge

This area relates to the inner spiritual areas of your life and is associated with grounding, knowledge and wisdom.

Enhance with

- Greens and blues
- Owls, elephants
- Meditation/yoga area
- Plants to represent growth
- A Buddha statue, symbolic of wisdom and knowledge and stimulating the unconscious to become more receptive to learning

Career

This area concerns your job and career success. Enhance this area if you would like to get a better job or get a promotion.

Enhance with

- Black and dark blues
- Wavy, curvy, asymmetrical or undulating shapes
- Fountains or other water features
- Reflective surfaces
- Frogs, fish, turtles

Helpful People and Travel

This area relates to synchronicity, being in the right place at the right time, networking, and lucky encounters. It is also associated with mentors and helpful people in your life (doctor, lawyer, travel agent). This area also relates to travel you do or desire to do.

Enhance with

- Grey, black, and white
- Round and oval shapes
- Stone and metal sculptures
- Metal objects
- Religious or spiritual figures associated with your own beliefs—cherubs, angels, buddhas, saints, gods, and goddesses
- Eagles (representing you soaring to new places)
- Statuary of modes of travel (cars, planes, trains)
- Garden décor you purchased on a trip
- Exotic flowers
- Bird house, bird feeder, birdbath

Statuary and Ornaments

The statuary and ornaments you place in your garden can have great significance. Be conscious of where you locate them so they act as enhancements to each Bagua area.

Choose your garden sculpture carefully. Remember that anything that is friendly is preferred to something that is threatening or hostile. Angels are wonderful because they give off positive energies. Scary-looking gargoyles or statues with missing limbs are not the best choices to create a serene atmosphere. Sculptures of fierce-looking animals such as lions or fu dogs are best placed near the entrance of your home as guardians.

Let people who are exploring your garden discover surprises—pieces of statuary or ornaments hidden among your flowers.

Ponds and Water Features

Water has always been synonymous with power. The ancient Chinese believe that water is the ultimate wealth symbol and that by harnessing the flow of water in just the right way, we can be assured of a lifetime of wealth and abundance. That is why you often see aquariums at the front of Chinese restaurants.

Ponds in gardens are excellent Feng Shui enhancements. Moving water brings prosperity and good luck. The sound and motion of moving water activates Chi and creates a relaxing atmosphere.

Become a Helpful Person yourself and participate in community events and neighborly activities.

- Visit your local farmers' market
- Compliment a neighbor on his garden
- Share a cutting or division with a friend
- Plant a Row for the Hungry or share your garden's bounty with a local shelter
- Volunteer at a school garden club
- Join your local garden club or botanic garden

Your water feature, whether a pond or swimming pool, should be in proportion to the size of your house and the size of the land the house is on. The shape of the body of water is best if it resembles shapes found in nature. Irregular, kidney, and rounded shapes are considered the most auspicious.

Placement of your water feature is a critical element in wealth enhancement. Lucky wealth areas for a pond or water feature are in the areas of your yard associated with prosperity, career, and family. You probably won't choose to have a pond at your front door, but placing a water fountain or birdbath is an option to consider.

However, don't worry if your pond is not located in one of the auspicious areas of the Bagua. You can cure these situations. For example, if your pond is located in your Fame area where the element is fire (and, of course, water puts out fire), add more fire to this area—tall red plants; animals such as turtles, frogs, and the fish in your pond; and statuary.

Following are lists of common plants and flowers that can be used to enhance each area of the Bagua. It is not all-inclusive and is meant only as a guide. It is not necessary to plant each area of your yard with the associated Bagua color. Plant only flowers that you love and that feel right for you. (And remember that plants grow differently in each climate zone. A flower that thrives in one area of the country may struggle somewhere else.)

Prosperity

Annuals		Perennials	
Sun	Shade	Sun	Shade
Ageratum	Browalia	Aster	Johnny jump-up
Alstromeria	Coleus	Butterfly bush	Torenia
Alyssum	Fuschia	Campanula	Violet
Aster	Impatiens	Canterbury bells	
Blue salvia	Pansy	Chrysanthemum	
Bluebells	Torenia	Columbine	
Cornflower		Delphinium	
Geranium		Hydrangea	
Globe amaranth		Iris	
Larkspur		Jacob's ladder	
Lisianthus		Lavender	
Lobelia		Lupine	
Morning glory		Money plant	
Petunia		Purple coneflower	
Purple fountain grass		Purple ice plant	
Verbena		Veronica	
Vinca		Wisteria	

Fame and Reputation

Annuals		Perennials	
Sun	Shade	Sun	Shade
Celosia	Begonia	Aster	Astilbe
Cosmos	Buschia	Bee balm	Bee balm
Four o'clocks	Coleus	Bird of paradise	Celosia
Gazania daisy	Impatiens	Blanket flower	Coral bells
Geranium		Canna	Cosmos
Gerbera daisy		Chinese lantern	Gazania daisy
Hollyhock		Chrysanthemum	Geranium
Nasturtium		Dianthus	Sunflowers
Nicotiana		Gladiolus	
Petunia		Hibiscus	
Portulaca		Hollyhock	
Purple fountain grass		Jupiter's beard	
Salvia		Liatris	
Snapdragon		Penstemon	
Sunflowers		Poppy	
Verbena		Prairie coneflower	
Zinnia		Red hot poker	
		Roses	

Relationships

Annuals		Perennials	
Sun	Shade	Sun	Shade
Alstromeria	Begonia	Aster	Astilbe
Alyssum	Coleus	Bee balm	Bee balm
Cleome	Fuschia	Clematis	Bleeding heart
Cosmos	Impatiens	Columbine	Bugbane
Geranium		Dianthus	Calladium
Gerbera daisy		Foxglove	Coral bells
Hollyhock		Hibiscus	Foxglove
Lisianthus		Hollyhock	
Nicotiana		Jupiter's beard	
Petunia		Liatris	
Snapdragon		Peony	
Sweet pea		Phlox	
Verbena		Poppy	
Vinca		Rose of Sharon	

Family

Annuals		Perennials	
Sun	Shade	Sun	Shade
Bamboo	Caladium	Corydalis	Astilbe
Bells of Ireland	Coleus	Chrysanthemum	Ferns
Grasses	Elephant's ears	Fruit trees	Ginger
Herbs	Impatiens	Hens and chicks	Hosta
Hollyhock	Shamrock	Hollyhock	Irish moss
Nicotiana		Hydrangea	Ivy
Potato vine		Lilac	Lady's mantle
Zinnia		Sedum	Pachysandra
		Thyme	Solomon's seal

Health

Annuals		Perennials	
Sun	Shade	Sun	Shade
Calendula	Coleus	Achillea (yarrow)	Corydalis
Dahlia	Impatiens	Black-eyed Susan	Foxglove
Gazania daisy	Pansy	California poppy	
Gerbera daisy		Columbine	
Marigold		Coneflower-yellow	
Nasturtium		Coreopsis	
Petunia		Chrysanthemum	
Snapdragon		Daylily	
Sunflowers		Evening primrose	
Zinnia		Forsythia	
		Hollyhock	
		Ice plant	
		Iris	
		Loosestrife	
		Red hot poker	

Children and Creativity

Annuals		Perennials	
Sun	*Shade*	*Sun*	*Shade*
Ageratum	Begonia	Baby's breath	Astilbe
Alstromeria	Browalia	Bartered bride	Bleeding heart
Alyssum	Coleus	Calla Lily	Caladium
Campanula	Impatiens	Camellia	Coral bells
Cleome	Nicotiana	Candytuft	Cyclamen
Cosmos	Pansy	Clematis	Foxglove
Dahlia		Coneflower	Goat's beard
Geranium		Coral bells	Lily of the valley
Lobelia		Daisy	Shooting star
Marigold (white)		Dianthus	Sweet woodruff
Moonflower		Flax	Trillium
Morning glory		Gladiolus	
Petunia		Honeysuckle	
Queen Anne's lace		Iris	
Salvia		Lilac	
Stock		Mexican pinwheel	
Sunflowers		Obedient plant	
Verbena		Phlox	
Vinca		Poppy	

Skills and Knowledge

Annuals		Perennials	
Sun	Shade	Sun	Shade
Aster	Browalia	Aster	Corydalis
Bachelor's Buttons	Lobelia	Balloon flower	Himalayan blue Poppy
Blue bells	Pansy	Bee balm	Hosta
Blue Salvia	Torenia	Blue flax	Vinca
Lily of the Nile		Delphinium	Violet
Morning glory		Iris	
Petunia		Lupine	
		Plumbago	
		Veronica	

Career

Annuals		Perennials	
Sun	Shade	Sun	Shade
Black potato vine	Browalia	Black mondo grass	Taro (Black Magic)
Chocolate cosmos	Coleus (Black Dragon)	Coneflower	Black cohosh
Elephant's ears	Pansy	(Black Beauty)	
	Violet (Black Prince)	Day lily	
		(Midnight Oil)	
		Hollyhock	
		Iris (Black Swan)	

Helpful People and Travel

Annuals		Perennials	
Sun	Shade	Sun	Shade
Dusty miller	Impatiens	Artemesia	Caladium
Licorice plant		Daisy	Lamium
Silver sage		Lamb's ears	
		Lychnis	
		Hollyhock	
		Honeysuckle	
		Mullein	
		Pussy Toes	
		Snow in Summer	
		Yarrow	

When placing Feng Shui enhancements, it is not necessary to fill your house with Chinese objects and symbols. You can tailor your visual enhancements to your own personal style. For instance, instead of a wealth frog to symbolize prosperity, you may use a framed dollar bill or whatever symbolizes prosperity to you personally. If you would like to use the Chinese symbolism, the following is a list of commonly used items.

Bagua mirror A Bagua mirror is a tool that redirects negative energy back to its origin. Hang it outside over your front door to protect your home and family. This will prevent negative energy and any harmful influences from entering your home. Bagua mirrors are also a great remedy for quieting noisy neighbors or their pets.

Bells For thousands of years, bells have been used to ward off evil influences and announce good news. Bells are used in Feng Shui to symbolize the dispersal of negative energy.

Buddha Buddha is the embodiment of perfect wisdom, limitless compassion, and enlightenment.

> **Hotei Buddha** This traditional Buddha brings blessings and prosperity. He's a wonderful and auspicious symbol of good luck, happiness, and longevity.

> **Wealth Buddha** This Buddha holds a money pot and a peach. A large gold ingot sits among 18 smaller gold ingots. A string of pearls adorns the ingots. All are auspicious symbols of great wealth. The inscription is of the word *mun*—which means *full*—and says that your pot of gold will always be full of wealth luck.

> **Laughing Buddha** The Laughing Buddha spreads joy and happiness wherever he goes. He reminds us always to keep our sense of humor. His bag represents fulfillment of wishes or can also be the blessings of Buddha. Happiness is one of

the Laughing Buddha's greatest gifts. He looks relaxed and contented as he watches the world go by. We should all follow his example.

Carp   The carp has always been held in great esteem by the Chinese as a symbol of great wealth. You will often see them displayed in the homes of wealthy Chinese.

Cranes   Cranes are symbols of happiness, long life, and immortality and symbols of rejuvenation and wisdom.

Dolphins   Symbols of strength, joy, serenity, communication, and understanding. Images of dolphins promote a peaceful atmosphere.

Double happiness symbol   This symbol brings a double dose of happiness and is auspicious when it comes to activating marriage luck. If you are already married, it enhances your married life and brings wonderful and eternal love to your relationship.

Dragon   Dragons are the most powerful creatures in Feng Shui. Images of dragons in the house and at work symbolize success, prosperity, and abundance in wealth, luck, and health. Dragons are useful for maintaining good relationships with coworkers and your boss and gaining support from influential people.

Dragon turtle   Symbol of protection and support. The dragon symbolizes luck, the turtle long life; the baby turtle is a symbol of new beginnings. The dragon-headed turtle is the symbol of longevity in your home, especially for the head of the house. The dragon-headed turtle is also a powerful symbol of wealth, health, prosperity, and protection.

Elephant   Elephants are symbols of luck, strength, wisdom, carefulness, longevity, power, and high standards. The elephant is the Feng Shui cure for advancing your career and making your position within your company stronger. The elephant is a Chinese and Feng Shui symbol of sound judgment, strength, prudence, and energy.

Fish   Fish symbolize wealth and prosperity.

Frogs   The three-legged frog attracts wealth and success. Place the frog near your front door so money will only come in and not leave your premises

Gourd   The Precious Gourd, an ancient Chinese symbol of longevity, protects from evil and negative energy. It is used to attract good fortune. The Precious Gourd is also the emblem for the figure 8, which holds great power in Feng Shui and Chinese symbolism. The Precious Gourd is a wonderful talisman for protection at home or on a journey. Hang it from doors or windows, at the side of your bed, above the office desk, or inside a vehicle.

Healing stones   Rose quartz is known for its healing powers, and because it is usually associated with love, it can bring both health and happiness. The amethyst is a very powerful crystal that can be placed in a sick person's room to aid the healing process.

Kuan Yin   Kuan Yin (Lady Buddha) is believed to help with healing. Placed in a room, she is said to cleanse the environment of negative influences (such as disruptive issues, illness, and arguments). Kuan Yin is the eternal protector of all woman and children. She also represents universal compassion and love and is said to enhance fertility.

Lucky Bamboo

Lucky Bamboo's botanical name is *Dracaena*. Lucky Bamboo is an excellent way to attract positive Chi energy and enhance its flow. For centuries, Asians have considered it to be a very lucky and positive symbol. It is said to improve Feng Shui and create a space where you feel safe and more energized. It brings not just color into your house, but also luck, fortune, and prosperity.

Lucky Bamboo is tough and resilient and does not like direct sunlight, making it ideal for areas of your home and office where you do not have a great deal of light. It is considered extremely easy to grow. There are a few simple things that you can do to provide it with the perfect conditions for a long, healthy life.

If your bamboo does not have roots yet, cut the stems off at the bottom about 1/4 inch with a sharp, clean tool. (Do not cut the bamboo if it already has roots.) Place your bamboo in a container, add stones or marbles, and fill the vase with enough water to cover the roots. Check the water level often. If the chlorine content in your water is high, it may cause the leaves to yellow. Use filtered or distilled water instead.

Beware of too much sunlight. Lucky Bamboo grows naturally under the canopy in wet tropical rain forests. You might be surprised at how little sunlight your Lucky Bamboo needs to thrive. In general, the more indirect the light, the better. If you see burning or browning on the tips of the leaves, consider that the location may receive too much sunlight at some point during the day.

Curly Bamboo: Lucky Bamboo only grows straight. To get the bamboo to curl, growers have to keep three sides in the dark, while one side has bright light. The bamboo grows naturally toward the light and it must be manually rotated periodically to create the curves. It takes an average of 18 months to make one curl.

Mandarin ducks   A pair of mandarin ducks symbolizes long-lasting relationships; they mate for life.

Mirrors   Mirrors are one of the most widely used remedies in Feng Shui. They are used to expand areas, reflect images, or bring the outdoors into missing areas. They can be used to reflect negative Chi away from you such as a noisy neighbor or unattractive building.

Money Tree

This plant is easy to grow, and it can activate Chi in your Prosperity area. It is believed that the money tree will bring you fortune and wealth. The five leaves of the money tree symbolize the five elements—water, fire, wood, metal, and water. It is said that to find a money tree with seven leaves is incredibly lucky.

Rooster   The rooster is a peacekeeping symbol. He helps counteract office politics, gossip, and backstabbing.

Spider   Descending on a thread from its web, the spider is a messenger from the heavens, bringing joy.

Turtle   Symbol of longevity, support, wealth, and prosperity.

Water features   Water symbolizes the flow of money (make sure it is flowing *toward* you).

Wind catchers   Wind chimes, flags, whirlybirds, and wind divas circulate Chi. They are especially powerful in your Prosperity area.

Meanings for Numbers of Stalks Lucky Bamboo

1	Fame
2	Balance, partnering, romance, relationships
3	Happiness
5	Family
6	Luck
7	Health
8	Prosperity
21	Very powerful all-purpose blessing

The
Chinese
Zodiac

Legend has it that when Buddha decided to leave the Earth, he invited all animals to meet with him to say goodbye. Only twelve animals showed up, the rat, the ox, the tiger, the rabbit, the dragon, the snake, the horse, the sheep, the monkey, the rooster, the dog, and the pig, in that order. Buddha rewarded each animal with a year in a twelve-year cycle to be celebrated in their honor. It is believed that the personalities of people born during a specific year will be influenced by the animal of that year.

Rat   Imaginative, passionate, wise, and intense
(2008, 1996, 1984, 1972, 1960, 1948, 1936, 1924, 1912, 1900)

Ox   Bright, inspiring, patient, and hard-working
(2009, 1997, 1985, 1973, 1961, 1949, 1937, 1925, 1913, 1901)

Tiger   Loyal, courageous, enthusiastic, and generous
(2010, 1998, 1986, 1974, 1962, 1950, 1938, 1926, 1914, 1902)

Rabbit   Shy, discreet, prudent, and honest
(2011, 1999, 1987, 1975, 1963, 1951, 1939, 1927, 1915, 1903)

Dragon   Active, healthy, dynamic, and brilliant
(2012, 2000, 1988, 1976, 1964, 1952, 1940, 1928, 1916, 1904)

Snake   Clever, opportunistic, reflective, and helpful
(2013, 2001, 1989, 1977, 1965, 1953, 1941, 1929, 1917, 1905)

Horse   Popular, noble, and enterprising
(2014, 2002, 1990, 1978, 1966, 1954, 1942, 1930, 1918, 1906)

Goat   Adaptable, gentle, elegant, and easy-going
(2015, 2003, 1991, 1979, 1967, 1955, 1943, 1931, 1919, 1907)

Monkey Intelligent, influential, and ambitious
(2016, 2004, 1992, 1980, 1968, 1956, 1944, 1932, 1920, 1908)

Rooster Obliging, pioneering, and brave
(2017, 2005, 1993, 1981, 1969, 1957, 1945, 1933, 1921, 1909)

Dog Loyal, faithful, and unselfish
(2018, 2006, 1994, 1982, 1970, 1958, 1946, 1934, 1922, 1910)

Pig Tolerant, steady, chivalrous, and persevering
(2019, 2007, 1995, 1983, 1971, 1959, 1947, 1935, 1923, 1911

Trees can create privacy, add aesthetic value and can be used to block the wind. They will create shade and reduce energy bills. Be sure to check the maturity size when deciding where to plant a tree.

Cherry	Fruitfulness
Cypress	Nobility
Elm	Combats stress
Oak	Attracts health and inner fortitude
Olive	Peace
Orange	Wealth, happiness, good fortune
Peach	Immortality
Pear	Sweetness
Pine	Longevity, fidelity, faithfulness
Plum	Compassion
Willow	Grace

Within nine months of your baby girl's birth, plant a cherry tree in your yard. Cherry trees strengthen feminine energy. For a boy, plant a pine tree. Have the baby present when you are planting, and state your intention to encourage the tree's support through their lives.

The Chinese regard the peony as the flower of riches and honor. It is a Yang flower that symbolizes love, affection, and feminine beauty. If you are a single woman or a mother of a single female whom you wish to fall in love, hang a picture of a peony outside the bedroom door to attract romance.

The chrysanthemum is associated with the life of ease in the Chinese culture. Bright yellow is the most auspicious chrysanthemum color. The plum flower and plum tree are symbolic of good fortune, purity, and longevity.

The lotus plant is symbolic of peace, hope, and contentment. They are a great flower to use if you have a water feature in your yard.

The narcissus, hyacinth, daffodil, and lily are all very auspicious bulb plants. The Chinese consider the bulb to be buried gold.

Amaryllis - pride

Bamboo - longevity

Bellflower - gratitude

Chrysanthemum - endurance

Daffodil - buried gold

Daisy - innocence and beauty

Fern - fascination and sincerity

Forget-me-not - true love

Forsythia - optimism, joy, and vitality

Fuschia - good fortune

Gardenia - secret untold love, strength

Geranium - durability for overcoming obstacles

Hibiscus - abundance, wealth, and fame

Hollyhock - promotes fertility

Honeysuckle - generosity, devoted affection

Hydrangea - achievement

Ivy - patience and friendship

Juniper - tolerance

Larkspur - laughter

Lilac - first love

Lotus- peace, enlightenment

Orchid - rare beauty, strength, and bravery

Peony - love, affection

Rhododendron - delicacy

Roses

    Red - passion

    Coral - desire

    Pink - grace

    White - worthiness

    Yellow - joy

Tulip - love and devotion

Wisteria – beauty

A Guide to Chinese Horoscopes, D.J. Burns, New York, NY, Barnes & Noble Books, 2001.

Clear Your Clutter With Feng Shui, Karen Kingston, New York, NY. Broadway Books, 1998.

Feng Shui in the Garden, Richard Webster, St. Paul, MN. Llewellyn Publications, 1999.

How to Grow Fresh Air, Dr. B.C. Wolverton, New York, NY. Penguin Books, 1997.

Quick Feng Shui Cures, Sarah Shurety, New York, NY, Hearst Books, 1999.

Success With Feng Shui in Your Garden, Gunther Sator, London, England, Merehurst Limited, 1999.

The Feng Shui Garden, Gill Hale, Pownal, Vermont, Storey Books, 1998.

The Western Guide to Feng Shui: Creating Balance, Harmony, and & Prosperity in Your Environment, Terah Kathryn Collins, Carlsbad, CA, Hay House, Inc. 1996.

The Western Guide to Feng Shui for Prosperity, Terah Kathryn Collins, Carlsbad, CA, Hay House, Inc. 2002.

BOOK ORDERS

Fax orders: 303-433-9693. Send this form.

Telephone orders: 303-458-1255.

Email orders: orders@homeandgardenfengshui.com

Mail orders: Home and Garden Feng Shui LLC
                  2510 Raleigh Street, Denver, CO 80212

Please send me the following books:

	QTY	TOTAL
Feng Shui for your Home and Garden:		
An Easy Guide for Everyone ($14.95)	____	$_____
Sales Tax:		
Colorado residents add 7.2%		$_____
Shipping:		
US: $4.00 for first book and		$_____
$2.00 for each additional book	____	$_____
International:		
$9.00 for first book and		$_____
$5.00 for each additional book	____	$_____
Total		$_____

Payment:

US Check, ____ or Money order enclosed ____

Credit card: Visa ____ Master Card ____

Card number: _____

Exp. Date: ____ Name on Card: _____

Signature of Card holder: _____